P9-ART-500

Hollywood Moments

Hollywood Moments

Text and Photographs by Murray Garrett

Harry N. Abrams, Inc., Publishers

Page 2:
Richard Burton, 1968

**Elizabeth Taylor and
Mike Todd making an
entrance at the
premiere of** Raintree
County, **Beverly Hills,
1957**

Contents

Dedication and Acknowledgments

Anyone who has written a book knows how many people have been there with him along the way, helping, encouraging, and cheering him on, from his earliest years to the moment he finally holds the book in his hands. And so, with love and gratitude, I dedicate this book first of all to these treasured people: to my parents, Freda and Samuel Glassberg, whose love, "golden rule" principles, and work ethic set the standard for my own life; to my friend and sister Pearl, the family brain, and her husband, Leo; to my wife of fifty-six years, Phyllis, and our children, Marc, Judy, Richard, and our "baby," Eileen, who beseeched me to get started on a book and then, unfortunately, did not live long enough to see either of them completed; my dear grand-children, Niki and Andy Nield, Amy Weisinger, and the latest edition, Celeste Garrett, all of whom keep Papa smiling.

I also dedicate this book to two wonderful friends and business partners, the late Gene Howard, and Leo Monahan. Gene Howard, my friend in Heaven, was the most talented person I ever knew. Gene started out as a big-band singer with Gene Krupa and Stan Kenton. After he left his music career to work in photography—which started out as a hobby for him—he and I developed a lifelong friendship. Eventually he and I formed a successful business relationship, called first Garrett-Howard, and later, Studio Five.

Marilyn Monroe and Betty Grable with Walter Winchell

My friend Leo Monahan was a brilliant graphic designer, and is now a world-renowned illustrator. Leo joined Gene Howard and me to form Studio Five as Art Director and Partner, and together we made Studio Five the leading photographic and art studio in Hollywood during the 1950s and 1960s.

I also want to dedicate my book to a number of dear friends. First, to Dan and Rita Paul, owners of the Washington Square Hotel in Greenwich Village, just a short walk from my publsher. Dan and Rita gave me a home away from home when I visited New York during the development of both my books. Second, to a bunch of kids I grew up with in Brooklyn: Bless you all for your contributions to a wonderful childhood and adolescence. I also want to remember my West-Coast friends, who grew up with me—and helped me grow up—in the wonderful, wacky business of Hollywood. Among these are Dr. Al and Teri Frank, Army Archerd, Johnny Grant, Freddie Amsel, Len and Doris Kaufman, Irv and Barbara Kaze, Mike Dougherty, Henry McCann, Ben and Peggy Irwin, Frank and Pat Liberman, Martin and Moneta Lynn, Mike and Dodie Newberger, Lee Hazlewood, Aleon and Vonne Bennett, and Joe Bleeden.

In the creation of the book itself, I have been fortunate to have another opportunity to work with the same team that made my first book, *Hollywood Candid: A Photographer Remembers,* a success. First of all, I would like to thank John Crowley, Head of the Department of Photographs and Permissions at Harry N. Abrams, Inc. It would take another book to express my appreciation to John, who, from the beginning, believed in me, my photographs, and my ideas strongly enough not only to be my enthusiastic advocate, but also to walk me through the publishing minefield, not just once, but twice. I also want to thank Elaine Stainton, Senior Editor at Abrams. I have collaborated with editors most of my professional life, but I have never enjoyed working with any of them as much as I have with Elaine. Her respect for my work, combined with her low-pressure manner of making the right decisions and getting the job done, are remarkable assets that I shall always remember. Third, but not least, I want to express my warm thanks to Myrna Lieberman, who helped me create a database for my archive of photographs, many of which were shot before she was born. I am grateful for her talent, assistance, patience, and devotion to helping me transform corrugated cartons filled with negatives, prints, clippings, notes, and memories into two published books. Myrna is my niece through marriage and now my good friend through hard work.

Finally, to my photography teachers Bernard Hertzig, Lester Feinstein, and Mel Rosenthal; photographers Eileen Darby, Lisa Larsen, Lenny Ufland, Jimmy Sileo, Henry Rappe, Ben Mancuso, Bob Landry, J. B. Scott, Alan Grant, Chuck Clumb, and Gene Howard: my warmest thanks for a lifetime of excitement and pleasure.

Murray Garrett

Ava Gardner on the air at NBC Studio, 1951

Overleaf:
Debbie Reynolds and her date at a benefit dinner, 1954

9

Debbie Reynolds on Murray Garrett

Howard Strickling was the head of public relations at MGM, the studio that first signed me as a teenager. I remember Mr. Strickling telling me that he considered Murray Garrett a "photographer's photographer." Not only did he cover Hollywood for some of the best-known publications in the world, he was also trusted by some of the biggest names in town—people like Bob Hope, Frank Sinatra, Bing Crosby, Loretta Young, Charles Laughton, and Barbara Stanwyck. Murray did private photographic work for every one of them.

What I recall most vividly about Murray was how quickly and efficiently he did his job. Whether he was working at one of my Thalian parties in Beverly Hills or shooting a layout of me at my home in Burbank, I was always impressed by how unobtrusive, pleasant, and accommodating Murray was, to me and to all of his subjects.

On my coffee table at home is a copy of *Hollywood Candid: A Photographer Remembers*, Murray's first book, which is filled with simply wonderful photographs of the people I grew up with in Hollywood. I am sure you will enjoy his second book, *Hollywood Moments*, which is filled with more great photos and anecdotes about Hollywood in its heyday.

Sincerely,

Debbie Reynolds

Introduction

Photojournalists, rarely, if ever, find themselves in front of a camera. We live *behind* the camera. Like most other journalists, I was thrilled to get a byline or photo credit when I first started out. However, as time passed, I married and started raising a family, and reality set in. You simply can't take a byline or a photo credit to the grocery. But here I am, almost sixty years from the beginning of my career, the author of a book that has been reviewed favorably and featured in a number of national publications, including *American Heritage Magazine* (with a six-page layout), *People*, *Entertainment Weekly*, *Esquire*, *Photographic*, and *Playboy*.

The thought that I would ever find myself writing the introduction to a second book never entered my mind when I first set out to publish my photographs. But my first book, *Hollywood Candid: A Photographer Remembers*, was a bigger success than I had ever expected. The first printing was sold out ten weeks after its release; the second printing was more than twenty percent sold prior to its arrival from the printer. This was the best holiday gift I ever received.

Looking back, the year since the publication of *Hollywood Candid* has been an exciting, heaven-sent dream. As I approached my seventy-fifth birthday, I was in excellent health, and feeling like the proverbial kid in the candy store—with a free pass! The experience

One of the great ladies of Hollywood, Mary Pickford, and her husband, Buddy Rogers

of becoming a successful author; of being interviewed by journalists from newspapers, magazines, and on radio and television; of being booked for speaking engagements and book signings; of signing autographs for fans, is simply impossible to describe.

As a native of Brooklyn, New York, I was thrilled and humbled when my hometown newspapers reviewed the book. The New York *Daily News* did a two-page centerfold feature on it; and the *New York Times* gave it a favorable review in their Sunday section. As a rule, art and photography books, let alone books by virtually unknown authors, are not reviewed at all. Discussing the success of *Hollywood Candid*, my dear friend, the Hollywood producer and writer Leonard Kaufman, said it all: "Murray, I wouldn't have dared write this script, not because you don't deserve everything good that has happened to you, but simply because Cinderella stories just don't sell anymore. Who would believe it?"

Now, as I embark on a new book, *Hollywood Moments*, I have a good feeling about publishing more photographs of the very special people with whom I was fortunate enough to spend much of my working life. Recently recovered negatives of such "old friends" as Barbara Stanwyck, Clark Gable, Peter Sellers, Ethel Merman, Shirley Temple, Judy Garland, and many others are in this book. But beyond the photographs, I learned something important from friends, interviewers, and people that I met at the book signings for *Hollywood Candid*. What nearly everyone told me was that what had made that book different from so many other splendid books of Hollywood photographs were the stories—my personal, anecdotal experiences with the larger-than-life characters who had made Hollywood great. These gave the reader a fresh, firsthand look at some of their favorite Hollywood stars from the Golden Era.

I hope that you will enjoy these special Hollywood Moments as much as I have enjoyed reliving them for you through this book.

Shared Moments

Some of my contemporaries in Hollywood didn't seem to understand that their access to the fabulous personalities of Hollywood was made possible only because they were photojournalists working for the leading publications of our time. Photojournalists were really the middle men between the stars and their public, capturing images of these "bigger than life" characters, to be reproduced by the world's press. Without cameras or note pads we couldn't get in. What was special was what we did for a living.

When I first arrived in Hollywood from New York, I was surprised at the informality of press photographers when they related to film stars. While covering theater in New York City, I don't recall photographers ever calling Frederick March, Fred or Helen Hayes, Helen. It just wasn't done. Yet in Hollywood, the photojournalists working for fan magazines, newspapers, and weekly and monthly periodicals all seemed to be on a first-name basis with the top stars. At first, I found this very intimidating. I just couldn't imagine myself face to face with Clark Gable, Walter Pidgeon, Greer Garson, or Katherine Hepburn . . . calling them Clark, Walter, Greer, or Kate.

In time, maybe over a period of two or three years, I realized how much less formal Hollywood was from the New York theater. Most movie stars, their publicists, and studios would actually encourage the press to use their first names. I wasn't particularly comfortable with that, because of the way I was trained to cover the New York theater. I unknowingly was developing a special identity with the stars, as the only photographer on the beat who addressed them as Miss or Mr. in front of their last name. I wasn't doing this to impress anyone, I was simply trained to address people that way, as a show of respect for people who had attained professional success.

I had another idiosyncrasy. I took notes, just to record some of the interesting incidents that took place in the course of my work. I would write a quick note to record what had happened and slip it into my camera case. Back at my office, I would save these in a file called "anecdotes," never dreaming that one day I would use them to help recall some of the details of my work for books about my days in Hollywood.

Please allow me to share some of these moments with you. I hope you enjoy them for the first time, as much as I have enjoyed reliving them for this book.

Knockouts

Sometimes I think that first and foremost Hollywood is about beauty. But whether that is true or not, certainly one of the marvels of working as a photographer there was the astonishing beauty of some of the ladies.

Loretta Young at a benefit for Catholic charities at the Beverly Hills Hotel

On this occasion, I was trying to do my job, which was to provide Louella with shots of all her guests. But Oleg and Grace purposely kept looking off camera to discourage being photographed. The result is an odd composition. But, it was impossible to take a bad photograph of Grace. She still looks wonderful. Later she relaxed and took off her glasses, and looked even more wonderful.

Grace Kelly and Oleg Cassini at a backyard party given by Louella Parsons

Elizabeth Taylor was, without a doubt, the most beautiful woman I ever photographed. In the course of her career, she appeared on the cover of *LIFE* magazine an amazing eight times. Perhaps Richard Burton described her best: "the most astonishingly beautiful, self-contained, pulchritudinous, remote, removed, inaccessible woman I have ever seen."

Taylor was born in London on February 27, 1932. My old boss, Bob Hope, once said that she was "the most beautiful thing to come out of the Depression." Every experience I ever had photographing Elizabeth Taylor was memorable. Whether I was covering a western costume party, which she attended with her first husband Nicky Hilton in the forties, or a visit to Disneyland that she and her then husband Richard Burton made in the sixties, I was always astonished by her beauty, and her hypnotic azure eyes. But, despite her fame, Taylor was a pleasant and extremely knowledgeable subject. She was bright, articulate, and if you knew what you were doing and behaved in a professional manner, a pleasure to work with.

In the year 2000, the Queen of England named Elizabeth Taylor a Dame Commander of the Most Excellent Order of the British Empire. During that celebration I was invited to London's National Portrait gallery, where three of my photographs of Ms. Taylor were hung in an exhibition honoring "Dame Elizabeth Taylor."

On her sixteenth birthday in 1948, Elizabeth Taylor celebrated by attending a charity benefit at the Beverly Wilshire Hotel. The event was an art exhibition and sale of movie stars' work, including one of her own, a small sculpture of a head entitled "Mona Lizzie." I took this shot of her holding the piece for Time magazine—long before Taylor became one of the great superstars of the twentieth century.

Opposite:

Taylor and Todd greeting Eva Marie Saint, who also starred in the movie, amid a crush of cameras

Below:

Taylor and Todd ready to sign the guest register

Elizabeth Taylor's marriage to producer Mike Todd was said to be her happiest. These photographs were taken at the 1957 premiere of her film *Raintree County*. She and Todd were married later that same year. Tragically, Todd was killed less than a year later when his private airplane, the "Lucky Liz," crashed in the Zuni Mountains outside of Grants, New Mexico.

Zsa Zsa Gabor was a world-class self-promoter. She could generate more publicity for herself than any star I ever photographed. This 1950 party shot shows just how newcomer Zsa Zsa cunningly worked her way into a shot with two well-known stars of the day, Danny Thomas and Esther Williams. Thomas and Williams were seated with Williams's husband, radio announcer Ben Gage when Zsa Zsa slipped up behind the unsuspecting trio and created a photo opportunity for herself, as well as for the press.

If you look closely at the expressions on the faces of her three companions of the moment, you will certainly agree that they were politely handling the intrusion by the Hungarian beauty.

However relentlessly Zsa Zsa promoted herself, she was smart as a whip, and no comedian was ever funnier. My partner, Gene Howard, and I started collecting "Zsa Zsa—isms" in 1953, when this beautiful and hilarious blonde came for a shoot at our studio on the Sunset Strip.

Zsa Zsa would deliver wonderful lines unexpectedly during what would start out as a normal conversation. No dumb blonde, she played her stunning looks and cleavage with an off-the-wall sense of humor that created more celebrity for herself than her sister, Eva, could manage. Eva, although she won critical acclaim on Broadway and for her television show "Green Acres," could never get the ink that Zsa Zsa did. When Jack Benny asked Red Skelton if he was going to use Zsa Zsa on his TV show, Red replied, "No—for two reasons. One, I think she'd steal the show; and two, my wife would think she would steal me!"

Zsa Zsa Gabor stealing a scene with Esther Williams and Ben Gage, 1950

Gene Howard and I had some favorite Zsa Zsa–isms. Here are some of them:

On Men and Marriage:

Personally, Dahling, I know nothing about sex because I've always been married.

Husbands are like fires. You see, Dahling, they go out when unattended.

Dahling, a girl must marry for love—and keep on marrying until she finds it.

I want a man who is kind and understanding. Really Dahling, Is that too much to ask from a millionaire?

I have never hated a man enough, Dahling, to give back his diamonds.

You know, Dahling, I am a marvelous housekeeper—Every time I get rid of a man, I keep his house!

Dahling, your question about how many husbands I've had—Is that including my own?

Dahling, you must understand, getting divorced just because you don't love the man is as dumb as getting married because you do.

Dahling, a man in love is incomplete until he gets married. Then, dahling, he is finished!

I never remember anyone's name, that's the way the "dahling" thing began.

Zsa Zsa dancing with actor Richard Webb, a great hunk of a guy who never achieved stardom. When he stopped by my office to pick up a print of this photograph, he told me that he had thought about asking Zsa Zsa out and then remembered who three of her husbands had been: hotel magnate Conrad Hilton, actor George Sanders, and billionaire Hal Hayes. That was enough to discourage him.

Kim Novak with
actor Gene Barry
at a Hollywood
nightclub in 1954

Two of the brightest female stars in the MGM studio galaxy were Ava Gardner and Lana Turner, who were close personal friends. These two beauties are seen here in 1952, at the height of their respective careers, attending the Ribbon Ball at the Beverly Hills Hotel.

The Ultimate Knockout: Marilyn Monroe

Opposite:
Monroe making an entrance, on the arm of studio executive Richard Gulley

Monroe and Donald O'Connor at the party for the Hollywood
premiere for *A Star Is Born* at the Coconut Grove nightclub

Monroe and Grable in the parking lot at Ciro's nightclub, ready to
make an entrance to a party for Walter Winchell (see pages 32-33)

Carrying a press pass opened the door to many historic moments. Because of my profession, I had the good fortune to be at Times Square in New York City, cameras in hand, for both VE Day and VJ Day, which signaled the end of World War II; I covered Eleanor Roosevelt while she was still the First Lady of the land; and I photographed Chuck Yeager after he became the first man to fly faster than the speed of sound. I also covered the 1960 Democratic Convention, at which John F. Kennedy was nominated, and my lenses were trained on the first missile launching from Vandenberg Air Force Base.

All of these were historic moments. But no single event stands out more prominently in my memory than the one that brought me and my cameras face to face with the two most popular pin-up girls of the twentieth century. This was at a party given at Ciro's nightclub on the Sunset Strip in Hollywood for Walter Winchell, who, during his prime, was one of the most famous and most feared columnists in the world. Winchell was honored by, among others, the two most famous blondes of all time: Betty Grable, the uncontested queen of pin-ups during World War II, and her successor to the title, Marilyn Monroe.

Everyone at the party knew that this was a once-in-a-lifetime Hollywood moment. For me, the real highlight was seeing how Marilyn Monroe deferred to Betty Grable, who had been the number one box-office attraction at Twentieth Century Fox when Marilyn had signed on as a starlet at that same studio. At the same time, Betty Grable, a terrific lady, was well aware of Marilyn Monroe's enormous success. Grable seemed as impressed by Monroe as Monroe was by her, and she treated Marilyn with genuine joy and respect. There was not even a hint of competitive jealousy. In fact she seemed to be saying, "Long live the queen!"

Monroe and Grable arm-in-arm with Winchell

Leading Men

Hollywood's leading ladies were probably the most glamorous creatures alive, but the leading men were remarkable, too. They were handsome, of course. But beyond this, many of them radiated an extraordinary personal magnetism.

Robert Taylor, one of the handsomest men ever to star in a Hollywood film, in the cockpit of his airplane

Opposite:
The incomparable Clark Gable, attending the premiere of A Star Is Born **with his wife, Kay**

Like a number of other Hollywood actors, including his friends Jimmy Stewart and Robert Cummings, Robert Taylor was an "aviator," as we used to say in the good old days. He owned his own airplane, which he kept at the Santa Monica Airport, and whenever he could get away he would head off to Santa Catalina Island, Santa Barbara, or San Diego in it just to relax. Once I had the pleasure of being with him at the airport and hearing him speak of his joy at being "up in the clouds," away from the pressures of life at MGM. It was easy to see how much he loved flying, something that clearly ranked very high on his list of things to do.

Burton on the set of The Robe, **in costume for his role as Marcellus, with co-star Jean Simmons**

Richard Burton was born Richard Jenkins, Jr. in Pontrhydfen, South Wales, in 1925 and later changed his name to Burton, a name he borrowed from a professor at school. Burton's film career started in London at about the same time that I became a photojournalist in New York. I was an avid movie-goer in those days and I would try to catch every new Richard Burton film. When I met him in person, I found him to be a man's man, a polite, cooperative, and knowledgeable subject, who seemed very comfortable with who he was.

R

obert Mitchum, the personification of off-hand sex appeal

Robert Mitchum giving a jubilant bear-hug to Esther Williams at a softball game to benefit film industry-related charities at Gilmore Field in Hollywood in 1948. The two stars were thrilled to learn that they would be playing on Frank Sinatra's team, Sinatra's Swooners. The cause was so good that even the losers were happy.

This photograph of Robert and Dorothy Mitchum is unusual because when Robert Mitchum was out on the town, he wasn't always with his wife. Mitch, as he was called by his friends and people who worked with him, was one of the real free spirits in the film business.

On one hand, Robert Charles Durman Mitchum was a family man, who remained married to his childhood sweetheart, Dorothy Spence, for fifty-seven years. The Mitchums had three children, a daughter Petrina and two sons James (Jim) and Christopher—both of whom tried to follow in their father's footsteps as actors, but with little or no success.

On the other hand, there was the carousing Robert Mitchum. Early in his career he served time in the L.A. County Jail for smoking marijuana with two starlets, Barbara Payton and Lila Leeds. In the course of his years in Hollywood, Mitch was linked romantically with many actresses, but somehow his marriage to Dorothy always survived. This photograph of Robert and Dorothy Mitchum leaving a Hollywood nightspot is from one of the few times that I photographed them together. On this occasion, a new TV reporter on the Hollywood scene was going to seek an interview with the actor. He asked one of the old pro cameramen, "Who is that gal with Robert Mitchum?" —and got the classic burlesque answer, "That's no gal . . . that's his wife!"

Robert and Dorothy Mitchum

Opposite:

**Frank Sinatra and the batgirls for his softball team,
"Sinatra's Swooners": Virginia Mayo, Beryl Davis,
Gloria De Haven, and Betty Garrett at Gilmore Field
in Hollywood in 1948. The game was a benefit to
raise money for motion picture industry charities.**

Right:

**"Sinatra's Swooners" Virginia Mayo, Betty Garrett,
and Gloria De Haven**

Below:

**A big hunk of man: Victor Mature, with co-star Jean
Simmons, on the set of** The Robe

Three young stars of The Great Escape: **James Garner, Steve McQueen, and James Coburn at a private screening of the film in 1967 at the Directors Guild Theater for members of the Guild, film cast and crew, and their families**

Rock Hudson, a great favorite in the 1950s,
with Lori Nelson at a party

Class Acts

Hollywood attracted people of all sorts, some of whom were "class" personified. Here are some of my favorites:

Betty Grable, one of the sweetest-natured women in Hollywood

**Jane Russell with
Ruth Warrick and
Carl Neubert**

Jane Russell always was and still is a very unique lady. Born in a little town in Minnesota on June 21, 1921, she always preferred that small-town image. Jane was a tomboy at heart who loved blue jeans, loose shirts, and bare feet. As far as she was concerned, the sweater girl stuff was pure fantasy, and she thought her movie role as a "Howard Hughes-created sex goddess" in the 1943 film *The Outlaw* was a farce. Jane Russell's real life was, and still is, dedicated to WAIF, an organization dedicated to fund-raising for the almost 500,000 American children who are being raised in foster homes.

Here Russell chats with her friend Ruth Warrick, a leading lady who made her debut in 1941 in Orson Welles's classic *Citizen Kane*. With them is Warrick's husband Carl Neubert, who was one of Hollywood's most sought-after interior decorators. The photograph was taken at a party in 1948 to celebrate the opening of the film *Paleface*, in which Jane co-starred with another friend, Bob Hope.

Ray Milland was christened Reginald Truscott-Jones in Wales. Barbara Stanwyck was christened Ruby Stevens in Brooklyn, New York. They each starred in about one hundred feature films and ended their careers as TV stars, she with a hit series that still re-runs, "Big Valley" (1965–69), and he with two series, "Meet Mr. McNutley" (1953) and "Markham" (1959). Milland and Stanwyck were very good friends, great admirers of each other's work, and both were really a kick to be around. They called each other by their given names, "Reggie," and "Ruby." Milland, who had an extra dry sense of humor, explained this habit by saying, "We use our real given names out in public, so that our adoring fans will not recognize us."

Despite Stanwyck's fame, she was rather reserved. After her marriage to Robert Taylor ended, she continued to live in their house on North Beverly Glen Boulevard in the Bel Air district of Los Angeles. The house was just a few doors south of Sunset Boulevard, on the southwest corner of which, at Beverly Glen, there was a fire station. On an assignment to photograph Stanwyck at home, I suggested that we create a photo opportunity by paying a call on the firefighters to bring them some cookies and other treats. Her firm reply was, "No, I'd rather not." She didn't like the idea of PR as a "set-up," and she was uncomfortable at the thought of using the firefighters as stage props. Her last words particularly startled me: "I hate being on display. Attention embarrasses me."

Ray Milland and Barbara Stanwyck at a party following the 1953
opening of the Ice Capades at the Pan Pacific Auditorium in Hollywood

Ronald and Nancy Reagan, one of the classiest acts in Hollywood, at the 1963 Hollywood premiere of PT 109, **the story of the young John Fitzgerald Kennedy in the United States Navy during World War II. Nancy Reagan was the center of Ronald Reagan's life. Here she cracks her husband up with a funny quip.**

Ann Miller chats with actress Sara Shane and another friend at the Ice Capades opening at Pan Pacific Auditorium in Los Angeles, 1954

Dinah Shore seated with her husband, actor
George Montgomery, and their friend Frances
Bergen (Mrs. Edgar Bergen) at a party to kick off
the Dinah Shore TV show in 1952. The celebration
was at Ah Fong's restaurant in Hollywood.

ick Powell chatting with *Daily Variety* columnist Army Archerd at the 1952 Academy Award party at Chasen's restaurant in West Hollywood. Archerd, an old friend of mine, is still going strong. He continues to write a daily column, and he is very much a personality in his own right as Hollywood's most durable and trusted columnist.

Dick Powell and Army Archerd

They Were an Item

When Natalie Wood was sixteen, she had made enough money to buy a house in Laurel Canyon, in the fashionable Studio City area. I was assigned to do the first "home layout" of Natalie in her new house. I have had the good fortune to photograph some real beauties, including Elizabeth Taylor, Debbie Reynolds, and Pier Angeli, during their teens, but Natalie Wood was surely the most beautiful girl of that age that I ever focused my lenses on. When I went on the shoot, I was surprised by how unaffected and charming she was.

Natalie's career grew by leaps and bounds. She played the leads in *Marjorie Morningstar* and *West Side Story*, roles that made her a superstar. My cameras and I watched her become the toast of Hollywood. She dated the top leading men in town, including—as shown here—Warren Beatty, and the man who would later become her husband, Robert Wagner.

On this particular night in 1961 I had been assigned to take photographs at a premiere that was heavily attended by some of Hollywood's brightest stars. I was working with some of the most experienced photographers in Hollywood. They were tough old pros, absolutely blasé about working with their famous subjects, with whom they were on a first-name basis. Then Natalie Wood arrived on the arm of Warren Beatty—who had a reputation as a ladies man, to put it politely.

I was shocked to hear the comments coming from my colleagues. "What the heck is she doing with him?" one asked. Another said, "I'm going to call her mom tomorrow and tell her about Warren Beatty's reputation. That kid shouldn't be out with him!" Then I heard: "Oh, no! Can you believe that?" and "That's not right." To hear these hard-nosed veterans, who had covered Hollywood for years and knew all the gossip, reacting as if they were covering a high school prom in Nebraska and had just seen the preacher's daughter on the arm of the town ne'er-do-well gave me my first understanding of what a small town Hollywood actually was.

Natalie Wood stole America's heart in the mid-forties as Maureen O'Hara's seven-year-old daughter in *Miracle on 34th Street*. I had not fully understood the paternal instincts of my peers, whose hearts had been won over by a kid growing up in the movie business. So, on this particular night, Natalie Wood found herself in a cluster of overprotective big brothers with cameras.

Warren Beatty and Natalie Wood

Above:

One of the best items of all: George Burns and Gracie Allen

Opposite:

Mamie Van Doren and Ray Anthony, getting fit for a suit at Sy Devore's

On the west side of Vine Street, between Sunset and Hollywood Boulevards, across the street from NBC and around the corner from the West Coast's version of Tin Pan Alley and the network headquarters of CBS, was the location of Sy Devore's. From the late forties to the late fifties, Sy Devore's was the haberdasher to the stars. It was not uncommon to see knowledgeable autograph hounds hanging out at Devore's during business hours. One day as I was finishing a photo shoot at Devore's, I spotted Mamie Van Doren checking out a new suit being fitted on her soon-to-be-husband, orchestra leader Ray Anthony. The grin on Anthony's face says it all.

Actor William (Billy) Campbell escorts French dancer and actress Leslie Caron to a night of classical music at the Los Angeles Philharmonic Auditorium in 1959.

Leslie Caron and William Campbell

R ichard Egan was one of the most virile leading men in Hollywood. Many thought he would one day wear Clark Gable's crown; but, after starring in about twenty-four films, predominantly western and action flicks, he never came close. Susan Hayward enjoyed huge success in scores of films like *I'll Cry Tomorrow* (1955), *I Want to Live* (1955), *Valley of the Dolls* (1967), and *The Snows of Kilimanjaro* (1952). This red- headed beauty from Brooklyn, New York, was brought to Hollywood to screen-test for the role of Scarlett O'Hara in *Gone with the Wind*, which eventually went to Vivian Leigh.

Richard Egan and Susan Hayward at a party to celebrate the premiere for The View from Pompey's Head **in 1955**

Love and Marriage

"Items" sometimes become marriages. In Hollywood, some of these have lasted for decades; others have not.

Shirley Temple captured the hearts of film-going America at age three, when her career began with appearances in short films. All through the Great Depression, she was a phenomenal box-office attraction. The revenue from Shirley Temple movies helped Twentieth Century Fox to become one of Hollywood's major studios.

Once, when I was present, Shirley Temple was asked if she had ever believed in Santa Claus. In response, she recalled being taken by her mother to meet Santa Claus in a department store when she was about four years old. She said, "Everything was going fine. I was excited about meeting Santa and telling him what I wanted for Christmas. Then suddenly the whole Santa Claus thing blew up when Santa asked me for my autograph!"

As Temple grew up, it would have been almost impossible for her to have continued the success of her career as a child star. From 1947 through 1949, she made several unheralded films as an adult, then co-starred in the Fox film *Fort Apache* with actor John Agar, to whom she was briefly married. Temple remarried Captain Charles Black, a former Navy officer, and retired to enter local politics in Northern California. In later years she served as the U.S. Ambassador to Czechoslovakia and as an envoy to the United Nations. Captain Black's insistence on their leading a very private life almost makes this photograph a collector's item.

Shirley Temple and husband, Charles Black.
The ultimate child star grown up

Above:

Pat and Shirley Boone

Opposite:

John Wayne and his wife, Pilar

Pat Boone made about one dozen films, but his primary career was that of a recording artist, and no one was hotter than Pat Boone during the 50s and 60s. Here, Pat joins his wife Shirley (daughter of Country & Western legend Red Foley) at Pat's opening night appearance at the Coconut Grove in the Ambassador Hotel in Los Angeles in 1960.

Humphrey Bogart did not take well to intrusions, by members of the press, or even his friends. In this photograph, Humphrey Bogart and Lauren Bacall were at an industry soiree in Beverly Hills, when Bogey's old friend and drinking buddy, actor Van Heflin, approached. Just as I was taking this photograph of Heflin putting his arm around Bacall, I heard Bogey say, in a chilled tone, "Van, that's close enough." I wasn't too sure what was going on, but it seemed tense. In that kind of situation, especially one involving three brilliant actors—and particularly since Heflin was a deep-sea-fishing friend of mine—I thought it better to move on. Which I did.

Not too long after I took this photograph, I went fishing on an overnight charter in the Pacific Ocean just out of the Oxnard Keys with my friend publicist Ben Irwin and his client Van Heflin. At one point during our trip, as we were trolling our lines in the Pacific, I reminded Van of the incident with the Bogarts. Van's reply was to ask me, "What did you think about it?" I replied, "Frankly Van, I became very uncomfortable and just got the hell out of there." Van flashed that great smile, and mimicking my Brooklyn accent, said, "Yuh done the right thing, Murray." Then, without missing a beat, he asked me, "How much weight are you going to put on your line, when we go for halibut?"

Bogey, Baby, and Van Heflin

Hollywood has a history of "story-book marriages": Clark Gable and Carole Lombard, Robert Taylor and Barbara Stanwyck during the thirties and forties, and then it was Tony Curtis and Janet Leigh in the early fifties. No other couple, that I can remember during my career, ever received the concentrated, and almost all favorable, press attention that Tony Curtis and Janet Leigh received.

Tony Curtis was a New York "street kid," born Bernard (Bernie) Schwartz on the Lower East Side, whose father was a tailor. He seemed to have come from nowhere, and he burst on the Hollywood scene with a bumper crop of post-war actors that included Burt Lancaster, Shelley Winters, Piper Laurie, Hugh O'Brian, Robert Stack, Mitzi Gaynor, and James Arness. Tony, however, was wired differently than his contemporaries. He went after publicity in a straightforward way, even more so than Shelley Winters, who was the epitome of publicity seekers. For example, in 1948 Tony approached me and other photographers directly and asked, "Could you please help me with my career by getting me in as many pictures with other stars as possible?" I had never been asked that before, have not been since, by anyone, and if I had, I might have been offended. But Tony's homespun, warm, friendly manner somehow made it all right. I wanted to help out this fellow New Yorker if I could. I shot so many Tony Curtis pictures during that period that Bill White, then editor of the New York *Daily News* Sunday rotogravure section, where my work appeared regularly, asked my agent, "Why does Garrett shoot so many damned pictures of Tony Curtis? Are they related?"

Before getting together with Janet Leigh, Tony probably dated every available young actress in Hollywood. While on the town with his "cutie" for the evening, Tony would somehow manage to walk up to other stars, *either with or without his date*, at premieres, nightclubs, show openings, private parties, and bistros, introduce himself and create his own photo opportunity for the Hollywood press. During this orgy of publicity seeking, Tony was introduced to Janet Leigh. Janet was an already established star, signed to an MGM contract and wise to the ways of Hollywood. Janet seemed to "soothe the wild beast." Tony Curtis was out of circulation, and seemingly overnight, engaged to be married to Janet Leigh.

The coupling of Tony Curtis and Janet Leigh seemed perfect. Columnists Louella Parsons, Hedda Hopper, Erskine Johnson, and Florabel Muir referred to them as "The Kids."

Tony Curtis and Janet Leigh

They were invited to all the "Rat Pack" shindigs and were soon tight friends with

Tony Curtis and Janet Leigh

Frank Sinatra, Sammy Davis, Jr., Joey Bishop, Peter Lawford, Dean Martin, and Jerry Lewis and their spouses. Curtis and Leigh married and became the "darlings of Hollywood." They retained Rogers & Cowan, Hollywood's number one public relations firm, to make sure they kept that image. To add to the image, the Curtis-Leigh union produced a daughter, Jamie, but that wasn't able to save their marriage. Tony was off to Argentina to star in the United Artist epic *Taras Bulba*. There he fell in love with his nineteen-year-old co-star, Christine Kaufmann. That ended the marriage of Tony Curtis and Janet Leigh and began the marriage of Tony Curtis and Christine Kaufmann, which in turn rapidly ended in divorce.

If there is a happy ending to this sad story, it is that actress Jamie Lee Curtis, Tony and Janet's daughter, has a career that may equal or surpass the successes of either of her parents.

Dale Evans and Roy Rogers were considered the "King and Queen of the Cowboys" since their marriage (his second) in 1947. Until he married Dale Evans, Roy had been a two-fisted drinker and carouser. From the time of their marriage until his passing in 1998, Roy became a born-again Christian, and with Dale's guidance, contributed greatly to the aid of the world's needy. In addition to their charity work, the Rogerses adopted and reared close to a dozen children of all races and religions during their fifty-year marriage.

Roy Rogers and Dale Evans

Major premieres were always exciting, but the Hollywood premiere of *Show Boat* in 1951 was especially so. The biggest Hollywood stars were caught in the crush, and all of them were straining to get a glimpse of Ava Gardner, the star of the film, and her husband, Frank Sinatra.

Seeing these two together, it was impossible for me to imagine that they would not live "happily ever after," just as in a fairy tale. Ava and Frank were in the prime of their lives, so radiant and happy together, that they almost glowed. But sadly, this particular fairly tale did not last. Both Sinatra and Gardner admitted in later years that they were the love of each other's life. Unfortunately, their marriage was not able to withstand the pressures of show business life and excessive drinking. Their love for each other, however, did last. Sinatra carried a torch for Ava, and remained her long-distance friend and benefactor, for the rest of her life.

Frank Sinatra and Ava Gardner, one of the most tempestuous marriages in Hollywood history

In 1953 the french dancer and actress Leslie Caron, who had been discovered for American films by Gene Kelly, attended the premiere of the MGM film Lili, in which she starred with Jean-Pierre Aumont. She is shown here with her fiancé, Gordon (Gordie) Hormel, an heir to the Hormel meat-packing fortune.

Above:
Leslie Caron and Gordon Hormel at the premiere of Lili, **perhaps her best-loved film**

Opposite:
A radiant Ann Baxter attending an evening premiere with her actor husband John Hodiak

Judy Garland and Sid Luft at a party to
celebrate the premiere of A Star Is Born.
Behind them is Frank Sinatra.

Opposite:
Arlene Dahl and Fernando Lamas
at the Ice Capades, 1954

Above:
Elizabeth Taylor and second husband, Michael Wilding, at dinner

Right:
Taylor and Wilding at an art exhibition

Opposite:
Elizabeth Taylor and her first husband, Nicky Hilton, at a Western barbeque

Opposite:
Elizabeth Taylor and third husband, Mike Todd

Right:
Betty Grable and husband, bandleader Harry James

Fred McMurray and his wife,
June Haver

Opposite:
Jack Lemmon with his first wife,
Cynthia Stone, in the early 1950s

Family Ties

Maureen O'Hara and her brothers

Maureen O'Hara was said to be John Wayne's favorite actress. He knew what he was talking about, since she co-starred with him in at least five major productions. During her career, this gift to America from Dublin, Ireland, who was born Maureen FitzSimmons, appeared or starred in sixty films.

O'Hara kept her private life private. She often appeared at major Hollywood functions escorted by her two "kid" brothers, James and Charles FitzSimmons.

Clifton Webb lived with his mother, Mrs. Parmalee Hollenbeck, who would usually accompany her son to parties and premieres. Webb, who made a career of playing reserved, stiff, and even priggish characters, was actually relaxed and affable when he was with her.

Clifton Webb and his mother seated in the audience at a premiere in the 1950s

Left:
Dinah Shore and her daughter Melissa ("Missy") Montgomery attending a birthday party for Red Skelton's son Richard at the Skeltons' estate in Bel Air, around 1950

Opposite:
Red Skelton and fellow clowns Ken Murray and Ed Wynn at a birthday party for Skelton's son Richard (with Ken Murray). With Ed Wynn is Skelton's daughter, Valentina.

Right:
Richard Burton and his daughter, Kate

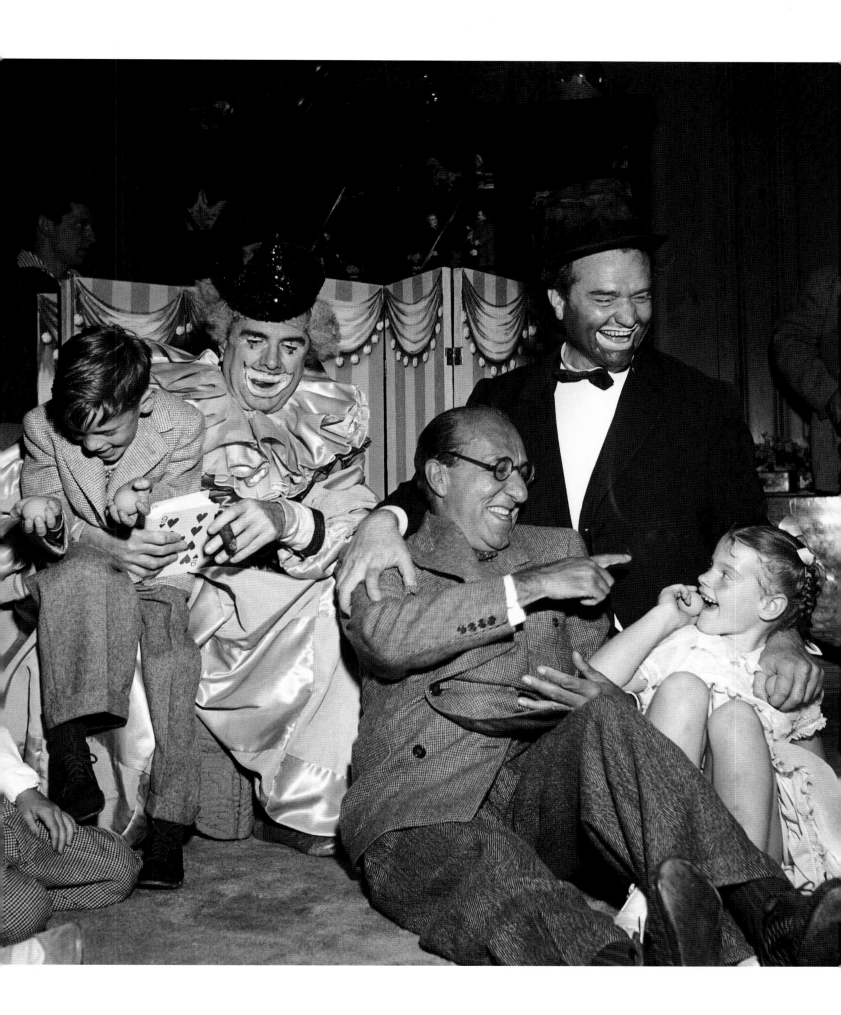

Working

Belafonte, always the perfectionist, in a last-minute rehearsal with his accompanist just before he opened at the Coconut Grove

Opposite:
Harry Belafonte in performance at the Coconut Grove

Harry Belafonte played the Coconut Grove nightclub in the Ambassador Hotel in Los Angeles during the mid-fifties. This shot, taken on his opening night, shows this great showman wowing the star-studded audience with his Jamaican rhythms.

Raoul Walsh was one of my heroes. As a kid going to films in Brooklyn I had liked his name and loved his work. I still remember the name "Raoul Walsh" emblazoned on the screen, giving him credit as the director of some of my favorite movies—*What Price Glory?*, *High Sierra*, *They Drive by Night*, *30 Seconds over Tokyo*, and *They Died with Their Boots On* were just a few of his films that I recall seeing as a teenager.

Less than a decade later, I found myself eye-to-eye-patch with this famous man— he had lost the sight of his right eye—at his office in Warner Brothers Studio, where I was to photograph him for a story to be published in *Time* magazine.

I was shown into Walsh's office, where I found him seated at his desk behind the largest piles of film scripts that I had ever seen. He was as impressive as any movie star that I had ever photographed. We made small talk for a minute and then this great director said, "Okay, young fellow, what would you like?"

I replied, "Your desk and the scripts are perfect."

Walsh then asked me, "Would you mind changing places with me, so that I can look through your camera?"

"Of course I wouldn't mind," I said as I handed him my Rolleiflex and sat down behind the piles of scripts.

"That's fine, just fine," Walsh said, and then added, "Key light me from up high, to accentuate my eye!" He was directing me and I didn't mind it at all.

When I left the Warner Brothers lot that day and drove back to my office I started grinning. Then I began to chuckle; and finally I broke out into a full laugh. Raoul Walsh, the great director, had set up all the scripts on his desk; he then had me sit in for him so that he could check my camera angle, and then he told me how to light him. I'd been had and I loved it. After all, he had really been nice. And he hadn't asked me to share my photo credit in *Time*.

Film director Raoul Walsh

You don't need me to tell you that David Niven was the quintessential Brit. Of all the celebrities I photographed perhaps only Cary Grant was more dignified, charming, gracious, and had such a zest for life—and mischief—at work or play.

Niven, a fine actor, who loved what he called, "the insanity of movie making," knew how to roll with Hollywood's punches better than any star of his caliber. He wasn't about to let anyone, whether writer, producer, director, or studio executive spoil his day. I think David Niven may have invented the saying "Don't get mad; get even." If anyone ever "got to" Niven, he never showed it. The ever-present toothy grin remained on his seemingly unperturbed face, while the wheels in his head would start spinning, planning his "getting even" pranks.

It was not uncommon to work on a movie set in which Niven starred or co-starred where strange things would happen after some incident had provoked him. A co-star's shoe could be missing, script pages might disappear, or, on location, a producer with a penchant for gourmet food could find a hamburger or hot dog with fries in his box lunch, while the rest of the cast and crew were dining on salade niçoise or cracked crab legs. And Niven was marvelous; he managed never to be near the incident as it played out. He would engage his co-stars, or others, in serious conversation regarding any topic ranging from the news of the day to telling stories about World War II and Winston Churchill. As the prank unfolded, he would never look up or change the expression on his face. No one ever knew exactly how these things happened, however, those in the know were pretty sure who the culprit was.

David Niven

ob Hope and Ava Gardner were friends, and they worked together often. Just to see the electricity between these two great talents was something special, and it resulted in some memorable pictures. These were taken at NBC Radio Studio in Hollywood in 1951.

Above:
Bob Hope and Ava Gardner on the air

Right:
Reviewing a radio script, February 1951

Opposite:
Hope and Gardner at a party, 1952

The One and Only

When I started in photojournalism access was everything. You could have the best and most modern equipment, the biggest car and the best darkroom facility, but if you didn't have access to celebrities to photograph, you had nothing. I never set out to get access, but I was just lucky enough to stumble on it through my work. The one thing that worked for me was that I immediately recognized how lucky I was to be getting the opportunity to work with these exceptional people. As a result, I also knew that my good fortune should never be taken lightly, abused, or sold out for short-term gain, in any way, for any reason.

One day in 1944, I received an assignment to photograph the singer Frank Sinatra in his dressing room at the Paramount Theater in New York. Sinatra had just left the Tommy Dorsey band, with whom he had become internationally famous as the male vocalist. His first gig as a single act at the Paramount was so overwhelmingly successful that he could not leave the theater, day or night, without a police escort. He was quite literally mobbed by women.

I didn't realize it at that time, but this occasion marked the beginning of a relationship that would last for years. Mr. Sinatra asked for a print of this photo, to which I gave a one-word reply: "Absolutely!" Sinatra furrowed his brow and with a raised eyebrow, said in his best Hobokenese, "You ain't sh_____ me now, are you?" I responded, in my best Brooklynese, "Trust me; I promise. I'll be here tomorrow with the print." And I was.

That incident turned out to be one of the most important turning points of my career. Although I didn't think about it this way at the time, I had treated my access to Sinatra with respect, and I let him know that I could be trusted.

Over the years, Sinatra and I would laugh about our meeting in his Paramount dressing room in those bygone days when mobs of Bobby Soxers kept him locked in the theater. Six years later, in the early 1950s, when his career had risen to new heights, *Time* magazine was doing a piece on Sinatra. The magazine was arranging to have a

Frank Sinatra in his dressing room at the Paramount Theater (1943–44)
with actor Sam Jaffe, writer Harry Hirschfeld, and a young musician friend

Left:
A recording session in a studio at Capitol Records in the early 1950s

Below:
Sinatra with his conductor and arranger Nelson Riddle

Overleaf:
Sinatra in his Beverly Hills office in the early 1950s

photographer cover Sinatra at his office and in a recording session. Sinatra questioned who the photographer would be. When he was told that the photographer would be Murray Garrett, Sinatra replied, "Yeah, he's a good guy. I knew him in New York."

The folks at *Time* were impressed. Later, when I thought this over, I was thankful that I had run that 8 x 10 glossy by the Paramount Theater that morning in 1944 and left it in an envelope marked "Frank Sinatra." Sinatra was, among many things, a man with a long memory. He was avidly loyal, providing, of course, that you didn't cross him. The fact that I was later given the opportunity to take the series of photographs of Sinatra at work was, I believe, directly related to the rapport that we developed when I delivered that photograph in 1944.

Above:
Sinatra recording

Opposite:
Sinatra in conference with his manager and close friend, Hank Sanicola, and Ben Barton, who managed the singer's music publishing companies

Fans

It goes without saying that the fans make

Hollywood. Without their enthusiasm there would

be no glamour to the movie business.

Oppposite:
Elizabeth Taylor at the microphone greets her fans over the P.A. system at a premiere on Hollywood Boulevard in the early 1950s

Below:
Fernando Lamas signing an autograph for a fan at the opening of the 1954 Ice Capades. Seated next to him is his wife, Arlene Dahl.

T.V. Hollywood

During the 1950s television became big
entertainment, and some of the Hollywood
actors began to work in the medium. This
was the beginning of new careers for some,
and the real heyday of others.

Oppposite:
**Jane Powell signing a fan's
autograph book at a premiere**

Right:
**One of the major stars of TV,
comic Red Skelton, on stage**

Ozzie and Harriet Nelson with Adrienne Ames and David Brian

Two of the great stars of TV were Ozzie Nelson and Harriet Hilliard. They began with a radio show, "The Nelsons," which became "The Adventures of Ozzie and Harriet" on TV and ran from 1952 through 1965. They played the real-life parents of rock star Ricky and actor David Nelson.

In this photo, Ozzie and Harriet are seated at rinkside for the 1955 Ice Follies, with their friends actress Adrienne Ames and her husband David Brian, whose star was rising following his co-starring role in *The High and the Mighty*.

Mary Tyler Moore and Dick Van Dyke, who both won Emmys in 1963, were tickled pink for themselves and their show, "The Dick Van Dyke Show."

Mary Tyler Moore and Dick Van Dyke at a party to celebrate the Emmy Awards of 1963

When I first arrived in Hollywood in 1946, Lucille Ball was already an established actress, but she hadn't yet "arrived." She had been playing light movie roles in such films as *The Best Friend, The Girl Next Door,* and *The Other Woman.* Everyone in the business knew that Ball was talented and funny, but no one seemed to be able to find the right vehicle for her talents. It took television to make Lucille Ball a real star. Her television series, "I Love Lucy," was an instant smash and through it Lucille Ball and the series will live forever.

The world changed for Lucille Ball and husband Desi Arnaz the day that writer Jess Oppenheimer came to them with his idea for a TV series based on an American housewife and her husband, a Latino entertainer and orchestra leader and their best friends and neighbors in suburbia, Fred and Ethel Mertz. The entertainment world was changed too, once William Frawley and Vivian Vance were cast as the Mertzes.

The show was launched in 1951. "I Love Lucy" would be the first TV series not shot as live TV using traditional TV cameras, nor kinescoped, but photographed with multiple motion picture cameras, in front of a live studio audience. This change in the production was a landmark decision that still stands today, mainly because it assured all viewers of constant picture quality offered by 35mm film, as well as the ease of editing.

The "I Love Lucy" show was never ranked lower than third in its six seasons on the air. When the final segment ran in 1957, the "I Love Lucy" show had earned five Emmy Awards and was the only TV show to be canceled while it ranked as a number-one-rated show. This would happen on only one other occasion, with "The Andy Griffith Show."

Today the "I love Lucy" show is literally an institution. All one has to do is to use their computer, go online and research "I Love Lucy." It is safe to say that the "I Love Lucy" show is earning much more money today than the millions of dollars it originally earned for Jess Oppenheimer, Desilu, CBS, and its four principal stars.

Lucy's husband, orchestra leader Desi Arnaz was born in Cuba on January 19, 1917. Up until the launching of "I Love Lucy," Desi Arnaz was best known by nightclub audiences and the record-buying public, for his rendition of the song "Baba Lu" and for the Latin rhythms that he brought with him from his native Cuba. Desi also was a heavy drinker who abused not only alcohol but his wife as well, both verbally and physically, during their

Lucille Ball and Desi Arnaz. A night out in the early 1950s

turbulent marriage. Combined with their marital problems, Desi's proclivity for booze, beautiful women, and horse racing finally left Ball with no alternative but to file for divorce.

After her marriage with Arnaz broke up, Lucille Ball was introduced to comedian Gary Morton while doing a Broadway show. They went out for a "Midnight Lunch"—a meal actors have after an evening's performance. The theater goes dark, they take their makeup off, and they're back into street clothes. For Morton and Ball, it was love at first sight. After that, they saw each other constantly, and soon married. Gary Morton gave up his own career and moved west with Lucy, where he would make an occasional TV appearance or appear in a cameo role in a movie. Gary was Lucille Ball's constant companion, best friend, and manager. The two remained married until Lucille Ball died at seventy-eight in April of 1989, as the result of a heart condition.

As I look back, I realize that I never particularly enjoyed working with Lucille Ball when Desi was around. He was irritable, short-tempered, and often rude. Meeting them out on the town was much more pleasant, at least before the success of "I Love Lucy." In those days Desi, whom very few people knew (especially compared to his wife), was delighted to get any publicity. After "I Love Lucy" became a hit, Desi almost instantly became impossible. He now had the "power" to threaten and bully. If he had been drinking heavily, wise reporters and photographers, despite their love for Lucy, would avoid potential confrontations with the belligerent Desi.

Working with Lucy one-on-one, or with her pal, Bob Hope, for whom I worked for almost twenty-five years, was always a delight. These two great friends, who absolutely adored each other, were also two of the world's best comedians. Watching them carry on together was somewhere between pandemonium and a riot. Working with the two of them was an absolute privilege, and not really work at all.

Lucille Ball was totally professional in her work, and not for one moment did she ever make you feel uncomfortable. She respected the fact that the press had their job to do, and that what we did could be helpful to her career. I found very little change in dealing with Lucille Ball personally, at anytime during her career, before after, or during "I Love Lucy." Lucille Ball was simply one hell of a lady.

In costume for a benefit for St. John's Medical Center in Santa Monica in 1948

Barbara Hale was one of the nicest, friendliest, and most genuine of all of the actors in Hollywood that I ever photographed. She never lost one ounce of her Midwestern charm. So it was a great pleasure to see her win the role of Perry Mason's faithful secretary, Della Street, opposite Raymond Burr in the long-running "Perry Mason" TV series. Here is Barbara seated at a desk, reenacting her signature character.

Barbara Hale as Della Street

**Hoofers Laurence Harvey, Janis Page,
Milton Berle, Lena Horne, and Jack Benny**

Television sometimes offered some great photo opportunities. I took this picture backstage at NBC TV Burbank while covering a Milton Berle Show in the 1960s. Mr. Berle, in his usual gruff manner, suddenly said, "Hey, why don't you get a picture of the five of us?"—the "five of us" being himself and his guests that day, a group of real entertainment greats: Laurence Harvey, Janis Page, Lena Horne, and Jack Benny Hardly believing my good luck, I asked for a "time step" toward the camera in good "Chorus Line" style. They did it, and I got a great shot.

Chit-Chat

One of the most engaging sights on my beat as a photographer was simply seeing my favorite screen personalities just having a good time shooting the breeze. Here are some of my favorite shots of Hollywood conversation.

Lawrence Harvey and Marion Davies, two world-class charmers. Marion Davies was the life-long companion of William Randolf Hearst.

Leslie Caron and Shirley MacLaine

I have often noticed over the years that dancers—more than actors or singers—genuinely admire each other's work. At this party in the early 1950s, Shirley MacLaine noticed Leslie Caron seated at a table as she was walking past. Shirley promptly leaned in next to Leslie Caron to introduce herself and tell her that she loved Leslie's work. Judging from the delighted look on Caron's face, I would guess that a mutual admiration society had just been spawned between this delicate, French, brunette ballerina and the bawdy, blonde hoofer who captivated Hollywood upon her arrival from New York.

Ann Blyth, Joan
Crawford, and
Sonja Henie at a
Hollywood party
in the 1960s

Right:
George Burns and
Jack Benny were
great friends, and so
were their wives,
Gracie Allen and Mary
Livingstone. Here
they are, arm-in-arm
in deep conversation
at a formal Hollywood
event during the
1950s.

Opposite:
Heads together:
Joan Fontaine,
Lana Turner, and
Ava Gardner at the
Ribbon Ball at the
Beverly Hills Hotel
in 1952

Good Friends

Regularly covering Hollywood, from the forties through the sixties, Hollywood's top gossip columnists and their leg men became very friendly with me because I, unknowingly at first, was an excellent source of "twosomes," the filler items that the columnists would regularly add to their copy to let their readers know who was dating whom.

Some twosomes could turn out to be hard Hollywood news, signaling the breakup of a romance or a marriage. For the most part, however, they were usually pairings concocted for PR, either by a studio PR department or an independent firm. The night I covered singer Pat Boone's opening at the Coconut Grove was a star-studded event, but one table received more coverage than the others. This was because sexpot Italian actress Gina Lollobrigida was paired with the current Hollywood heart-throb, Rock Hudson—who was really there for PR purposes only. In this case, the two really were "just good friends."

Rock Hudson and Gina Lollobrigida seated together in the Coconut Grove nightclub for Pat Boone's opening in 1964

James Cagney and George Burns

James Cagney was one of Hollywood's great talents for over half a century. He probably was the only Hollywood star that I can remember who was adored equally by his public as by his peers. As a photographer, I wished that I had been given more opportunities to photograph him. After all, I, too, was a fan. However, Cagney was a most private person. He valued his home off of Coldwater Canyon, where he lived with his wife when they weren't in Martha's Vineyard. With all of the access I had in Hollywood, my cameras and I never got to spend any time with this particular man, one of my all-time favorites. Cagney, incidently, refused photo-layout requests in the most polite manner.

I caught this rare shot of Cagney sharing a table with two of his favorite people, George Burns and Gracie Allen (back to camera). Cagney gave me an approving wink as I moved up with my camera and a furrowed brow asking for permission. I savored that moment. Although I admired him and respected his privacy, I must admit that the photographer in me was always in conflict with my respectful self.

L was always fascinated by comedians. My mother had an off-the-wall sense of humor; my father could tell stories in just about any dialect known to man; and my own reputation with the kids in the neighborhood and in school was that of always being good for a laugh. If I ever had serious thoughts about being a comedian, they went right out the window after I started working as Eileen Darby's assistant. As soon as I saw the likes of Jackie Gleason cavorting on stage in "Follow The Boys," or comedians like Sid Caesar and Danny Thomas destroying nightclub audiences, I realized how fortunate I was to be an aspiring photographer who could be funny with audiences of eight people or less.

My fascination with comedians reached a new high on a memorable occasion when I found my lens focusing on Steve Allen, Louis Nye, Jan Murray, and Jack Benny in one of the dressing rooms at NBC Burbank. Here, these four masters of comedy are in the midst of a serious conversation about the news of the day during the turbulent 1960s. To be "a fly on the wall" overhearing four great American comedians discussing the tragedy of Vietnam and the abuse of drugs among our young people was a very special, and a not-so-funny, moment.

Steve Allen, Louis Nye, Jan Murray, and Jack Benny backstage at NBC

ollywood had drinkers and heavy drinkers—and then there were Tony Martin and Dean Martin. Stars like John Wayne, Errol Flynn, Frank Sinatra, Van Heflin, and Victor McLaglen—heavy drinkers all—couldn't compete with either one of them. These two handsome singers/actors were unrelated. Tony's real name was Al Norris and Dean's real name was Dino Crocetti. In their prime, their show-biz names could be found on the top of the charts in publications like *Cashbox*, *Record World*, *Downbeat*, and *Billboard*. Tony had been a hit as a singer some ten years before his pal Dino came on the scene in the late forties. With his partner, Jerry Lewis, Dean became part of the biggest act in show business.

I took this particular shot at the request of Frank Sinatra—himself a legendary boozer—who came up behind me at a party and said, "Hey, Murray, you're missing a great picture. Over at the bar are the world's two greatest drunks! I want a print for my scrapbook." Whenever Frank Sinatra made one of his infrequent requests I always followed through. So here is the photograph of Tony and Dino hoisting one at the bar, which I sent to Sinatra soon after.

Dean Martin was very open about his boozing. Joking around, he'd say, "I don't wear cuff links, these are curb feelers." When asked if he fell down often while drunk, he would reply, "Sure! It's the only rest I get!" Tony Martin, who drank as much as Dean did, did not make it part of his act or persona. My friends who still work the Hollywood Beat tell me that Tony gave up drinking several years ago and that now, in his late 80s, he still works. His wife, dancer/actress Cyd Charisse, considers him the crossword puzzle champion of Beverly Hills.

Tony Martin and Dean Martin

It is not unusual to see a superstar entertainer being met by a limousine at an airport. In fact, that has become the norm. Once while I was doing a still shoot on David Niven, one of the vice presidents at United Artists appeared to say that he had arranged for a "stretch limo" to pick up Niven's dear friend, Sir Alec Guinness, who was arriving at Los Angeles International Airport from London. Niven replied, "That simply will not do. Please arrange for me to personally pick him up. Alec Guinness is my dearest friend and a British treasure. I must be plane-side to welcome him." So it was arranged for the "stretch" to pick Niven up at the Goldwyn Studio before proceeding to the airport.

David Niven then got that devilish glint in his eyes. He furrowed his brow, as he turned to the vice president and asked, as he also turned his eyes in my direction, "Wouldn't it be a smashing idea for our photographer friend, Mr. Garrett here, to accompany me to the airport, so that we can we can greet my friend Alec properly?" My immediate thought was, what a coup! So that was arranged, too.

David Niven was not only a wonderful guy, he was also a brilliant actor and a great negotiator with a keen sense of public relations. Hence, this exclusive photograph of two dear friends, fellow actors, and fellow Brits at LAX.

David Niven and Sir Alec Guinness

Primping

For people who lived by their looks as well as their wits, actors in Hollywood's heyday had to be careful of their appearance, so I often caught a shot of show business personalities checking the mirror, adjusting their hair, having someone else do it for them, each a candid moment that says something about showmanship and professional pride.

Oppposite:
Jane Russell having her necklace adjusted before an entrance

Above right:
Virginia Mayo has her jewelry checked as she prepares to go on stage at a film-industry charity fashion show at the Beverly Hills Hotel in 1961

Below right:
Maggie Smith checks her compact mirror at the Screen Writers' Guild Annual Awards Dinner at the Beverly Hills Hotel, February 1954

Quick peeks in the mirror

Moments to Remember

Since I first began photographing people in show business, I have loved working with British actors, and I have been grateful for their civility and cooperation. A number of my favorite stars are British, including Charles Laughton, Elsa Lanchester, Richard Burton, and David Niven, but Maggie Smith is right up there. She is everything a great lady should be.

Maggie Smith has always exemplified a dignified and reserved demeanor. I was full of admiration for her calm, courteous manner during the pandemonium caused by the hordes of press at the 1969 Academy Awards, where she won the Best Actress award for *The Prime of Miss Jean Brodie*. Smith seemed to respect the fact that we were all simply doing our jobs; behind her lovely smile, one could imagine her thinking, "This, too, shall pass."

My friends in the press in New York tell me that they refer to Smith as "Ms. Cool." From what they tell me, when she received a Tony Award for *Lettice and Lovage* and when she was nominated for the same award for *Night and Day* and *Private Lives* she handled herself just as she had when she received her Oscar: with great dignity and just a dash of enthusiasm.

Maggie Smith

Peter Sellers was immensely talented, but he could be something of a handful. His agent, Charles Feldman—one of Hollywood's most famous—once said of his client, "The only way to make a film with him is to let him direct, write, and produce it, as well as star in it." The executives at Grauman's Chinese Theater on Hollywood Boulevard found that those words of wisdom were true when they tried to get this eccentric Briton's hand- and footprints in wet cement.

When the day came to make the impressions, Sellers arrived with his then wife Britt Ekland and immediately made it known that wet cement was "horribly messy" and to boot, he wasn't too pleased with the location he had been assigned. At that point, an executive from Grauman's stepped in front of my camera and told Sellers quietly that this event was an honor, not a publicity stunt. He added, "You are becoming a permanent part of Hollywood history." At which, Peter Sellers, brilliant talent that he was, smiled politely and replied, "Thank you, my friend. Let's get on with it." And we did, as you can see from these shots.

Peter Sellers and Britt Ekland at Grauman's Chinese Theater

Judy Garland at an
after-theater party
following the world
premiere of A Star Is
Born **in 1954, in which
she starred with
James Mason**

Columnist Louella Parsons's parties were usually small by Hollywood standards;
however, they were always attended by Hollywood's elite. After all, who in the film biz
would dare say no to an invitation from Louella?

In this photograph taken at Louella's home you see Jack Warner, from the studio
that bore his (and his brothers') family name. Warner, cutting the cake, is standing next

to Garland, who was the star of the just-released Warner Brothers movie, *A Star Is Born*. To her left is songwriter Jimmy McHugh—author of "I Can't Give You Anything But Love, Baby," "Don't Blame Me," and scores of other hits. McHugh was Louella's constant escort.

To get this shot, I asked Ms. Garland if she would join these two fellows for cake-cutting, and she graciously obliged. If you think that the look on Garland's face seems condescending to Mr. Warner, you are right, because it was. After the photograph was taken, Judy came up to me, smiled, and said in her low, sweet, vibrato voice, "Murray, please don't ask me to be near that S.O.B. again." I winked and nodded affirmatively. I understood. I never enjoyed being around Jack Warner and I'm not too sure that I knew anyone who did.

The star with Jack Warner at Louella Parsons's party

My first experience with Milton Berle, in the mid-nineteen-forties, was, at best, unpleasant. The encounter took place at the Winter Garden Theater in New York City, where Berle was starring in a show. My job was to photograph Mr. Berle with a visiting war hero, Major Chang of the Chinese Air Force. A leader in the "Flying Tigers," a group of American, Chinese, and British airmen who had banded together to fight their common enemy, the Japanese Armed Forces, Major Chang had been shot down and severely injured and burned. He was then sent to the United States for surgery and rehabilitation. He had been invited to attend the theater, and afterward he was to be escorted to Berle's dressing room to meet the star. The pictures I took were to used publicize the show.

Upon arriving at the stage entrance of the Winter Garden, I identified myself and asked to see the theater's publicity man, who soon arrived with major Chang at his side. It was quite obvious by the scars on his face that the Major had been badly burned. After a brief introduction, we made our way to Berle's dressing room. The press agent knocked on the door, and we were quickly admitted. Before the PR man could introduce Major Chang, Berle said brusquely, "I'm in a hurry; let's go." While Milton was setting up the pose in order to show his better side, I quickly put my gear together. Some of the flashbulbs available during World War II were of inferior quality, and unfortunately, my first two attempts to shoot the picture were thwarted by bad bulbs, as I explained to Mr. Berle and Major Chang. Finally, the third bulb fired, and I got a picture. I then uttered the perennial photographer's line: "One more, please." At this, Berle literally grabbed me by the nape of the neck and the seat of the pants and deposited me outside his dressing room. Assignment over! I apologized to the press agent, who said, "Don't worry about it. I gotta take this from him every day." Back at the darkroom, I found that I had one good shot— and a very bad taste—of Milton Berle.

Over thirty years of assignments that involved Berle from time to time, I never ceased to be amazed at the man's crudeness. He showed a complete lack of respect for everyone he dealt with, including his brothers, who worked for him and whom he regularly abused. At NBC Television the technicians and other support staff on the Bob Hope show and the "Tonight Show" knew that if they screwed up once too often, their punishment would be an assignment to work with Berle.

Milton Berle with Major Chang of the Flying Tigers

Quick Takes

Above:

George Raft with Rose Marie at the Ice Capades

Opposite:

A quiet moment with Bing Crosby

Rapt attention: Betty Hutton and
writer Norman Krasna on the town

Humphrey Bogart and actor Don Taylor
sharing a drink at the 1950 Redbook
Awards at the Bel Air Hotel

At parties Humphrey Bogart would always manage to single out an old drinking buddy to kick back with, have some serious conversation, and at the same time, keep their whistles wet.

At the Beverly Hills premiere of the film *Fiddler on the Roof*, I observed Topol, the actor who had played Tevye, the leading role, take this opportunity to have a serious chat with Kirk Douglas about a planned fund-raiser for theater activities in Israel. Douglas, who has always been an active philanthropist, and still is to this day, listened attentively, and then said "yes." In the world of show business there is more than one way to "capture the moment." Topol knew that and made his move.

Kirk Douglas and Topol

osalind Russell was a major actress of the 1930s and 1940s, starring in such films as *Under Two Flags* and *My Sister Eileen* during that period. Later in her career, she starred in *Mourning Becomes Electra* (1948) and *Auntie Mame* (1958). Her career included a stint at MGM. When she was asked how it was to be part of the studio's great roster of stars, she replied, "At MGM there was a first wave of top stars and a second wave to replace them in case they got difficult. I was in the second line of defense, behind Myrna Loy."

When I shot this 1966 photograph, Rosalind Russell was attending a party at the home of columnist Louella Parsons. Just as I took the picture, Russell's friend Ethel Merman (top right), who thought she was out of camera range, exclaimed, "Hey Roz, you're gonna get shot in Louella's backyard!"

Rosalind Russell and Ethel Merman at Louella Parsons's garden party

Marlon Brando always looked upon Hollywood as something of a joke. From the day he left Broadway, the theater, and the Actor's Lab, he knew why he was heading for Hollywood: It was where the money, the international fame, and the movies were. The moguls were calling with fantastic offers for him, and naturally, he responded.

Brando became one of the very elite group of actors who were referred to only by their last names—Gable, Garbo, Astaire, Monroe, Sinatra, to name a few. He was a loner who didn't care about taking part in most Hollywood events. I may well have been the only photographer ever to shoot a spread of him at home. Gossip columnists meant nothing to Brando, even Hollywood's two big ones, Hedda Hopper and Louella Parsons. He did not ever covet publicity; in fact, he disdained it.

Here, like two ships passing in the night at the 1954 Academy Awards, Marlon is seen backstage at the Awards ceremony cradling the Oscar he had just won for his starring role in *On the Waterfront*. Louella Parsons, in the foreground, was backstage to cover the event. She was completely ignoring Brando, acting as if he were nonexistent, while Brando in turn intentionally manipulated himself and his Oscar behind her, to avoid eye contact. Not a word was spoken between them.

Marlon Brando and Louella Parsons

Living It Up

Parties are a central part of Hollywood life. Some take place in restaurants, some at private homes. Some are benefits for charity, some are just for fun; some are big events, others are intimate gatherings. But big or small, parties are part of what made Hollywood what it was.

Jayne Mansfield began her career as a beauty queen: She was Miss Photoflash in 1952. In Hollywood Mansfield, who was not without talent or brains, had very tough competition in the person of Marilyn Monroe. I think Jayne's career might have gone better if she had not come on the scene in the Monroe era.

In this 1960 photograph, Jayne is seen dancing with former "Mr. Universe" and occasional actor Mickey Hargitay, her second husband.

Jayne Mansfield and husband Mickey Hargitay on the dance floor

Above:
Co-stars Gloria Swanson and a friend dancing the Charleston

Opposite:
Marilyn Monroe and Louella Parsons being seated at the Coconut Grove

To celebrate the triumphant premiere of her come-back film, *Sunset Boulevard*, Gloria Swanson threw a party at her house in Los Angeles that lasted into the wee hours of the morning. She and a friend delighted everyone in attendance by dancing the Charleston.

During the 1960s I was often asked to cover—exclusively —columnist Louella Parsons's private parties, which she hosted at her home in Beverly Hills. These occasions were like the parties that most of us have, informal gatherings with friends, food and drink, some music, and conversations about business, politics, and family. But there the similarity ended. At Louella Parsons's party, the food and drink probably came from a famous bistro like Chasens, Romanoff's, or the Beverly Hills Hotel. And although the guests on Louella's A-list would chat with each other about their children and their families like ordinary folk, the business conversations were different. They could involve moguls making multimillion-dollar deals, or a producer feeling out a star or director about working in their next blockbuster movie. The stakes were very high—and incidentally, the steaks were always aged, cured, and tender.

But the most amazing thing about a Parsons party came after dinner. It never failed that Louella's beau, song-writer Jimmy McHugh, would wander over to the piano to play some of his tunes, like "Don't Blame Me" and "I can't Give You Anything But Love, Baby." Inevitably, McHugh would be joined by some great star such as Dinah Shore or Judy Garland.

This photograph was made on an evening that Ethel Merman entertained after dinner. From my early days of photographing shows on Broadway I had been an avid Ethel Merman fan. To hear this woman sing anywhere was a thrill. But to hear Ethel Merman, using that remarkable voice that could be heard in the very last row of the highest balcony of any theater, belting it out in Louella's five-hundred-square-foot living room is one moment I shall always remember.

Ethel Merman singing for guests at a party at Louella Parsons's house. At left is Joan Crawford.

Gregory Peck wasn't on the party and premiere circuit. He never seemed comfortable around hordes of press that would frequent the major Hollywood events. Instead, he would show up at semi-private soirees, away from the public eye. Although he was always represented by top public relations firms, he didn't seem to have the same burning desire for publicity that most Hollywood actors did. In this photograph, taken in 1949, Gregory Peck is enjoying a cocktail at the Bel Air Hotel during a very elite party given by *Redbook Magazine*.

Opposite:
Marilyn Monroe and Lauren Bacall meeting at a premiere

Right:
Gregory Peck across the bar

Hamming It Up

Not every actor can ham it up, but the best ones at it were brilliant. In my career I took a lot of shots of inspired silliness; some of these were of classic hams—like Jimmy Durante—but others came by surprise.

I could almost tell the whole story in one sentence: Everyone loved Jimmy Durante. There are, however, a few things I'd like to pass on about this enormously talented, incredibly funny, gentle soul, simply because there was no one else like him. My friend Joe Bleeden, Durante's longtime publicist at NBC, would often say, "Being with Jimmy Durante is like being with Santa Claus. You are safe."

For example, picture this: Jimmy, Joe, and I are at the intersection of Hollywood and Vine at the peak traffic hour, waiting for the traffic light, which is as red as red gets, to change. Jimmy is very hungry and we're headed for the old Brown Derby restaurant, just half a block away. Jimmy asks, "What are we waiting for?"

I reply, "For the light to turn green, so that we can cross without getting killed."

Durante replies, "Are you kidding?" He grabs our hands and drags us across Vine Street. Cars came screeching to a halt, horns were blowing, Durante was waving and blowing kisses at everything in sight. And suddenly, lo and behold, there was a crosswalk where there was none! It was like the

The Ultimate Ham: Jimmy Durante peeking around the door

parting of the Red Sea! We crossed safely, to the complete adulation of all of the drivers and occupants of the vehicles who were waving back at Jimmy, blowing kisses, and screaming the words to his theme song, "Inka Dinka Doo." At the far curb sat one of L.A.'s Finest on his motorcycle, doubled over in laughter. If Bleeden and I had been alone, we'd still be in Jail.

Going to the races with Jimmy Durante at Del Mar track was a treat almost beyond description. Jimmy always traveled with an enormous amount of cash. It might be in his pockets, in an attaché case, or even in a suitcase! He was such a generous tipper that waiters and waitresses in the Turf Club would actually get into fights trying to get him to sit in their section. But Jimmy was not a good gambler. Many times (more often than not) Jimmy would have a bad day betting and in utter frustration bet "across the board" on every horse in the race. In a close race, as the horses would come up the stretch to the wire, as the Turf Club occupants were rooting home their nags by name or number, Durante would be frantically waving his fedora and screaming "Come on, *anybody!*" He just wanted to cash a winning ticket.

Once when I was shooting Durante at NBC, a young dancer came up to him to say that he knew Frank Sinatra, and that he would like to be a dancer on the "Jimmy Durante Show." Over and over the dancer emphasized that he was a "goomba" (Italian dialect for friend or countryman) and that he "knew Frank Sinatra." After listening to this for a few minutes, Durante replied, "I *know* dat you know Frank Sinatra. But does Frank Sinatra *KNOW YOU???*"

There was one way that Durante differed from most of the big names in Hollywood. He actually enjoyed seeing the tour buses that came through Beverly Hills neighborhood to show the fans where the stars lived, which most Hollywood people thought of as an intrusion. If you had the good fortune to visit Durante at home, and it happened to be at a time when one of the buses came by, you would suddenly see this unbelievable man— regardless of his attire, or who was visiting him—run out on the front lawn at the sound of the tour bus's air horn. He would stand there and wave and blow kisses at his fans. Then he would come back inside and say to anyone there who had not seen this performance before: "Hey, I gotta do dat. I love 'em. Dey've been payin' my celery all deese years."

No wonder everyone loved Jimmy Durante.

The great ham, with schmoos

Above:

**Rowan and Martin
with Nat "King" Cole**

Opposite:

**Jimmy Durante at
the piano**

This piece of madness took place in Nat Cole's dressing room in the Ambassador Hotel, just before America's favorite balladeer went on stage at the Coconut Grove nightclub during a fund drive for the March of Dimes. The madness concerned the loss of Dick Martin's pen. All Nat Cole had in his right hand was the pen top. As a result, comedians Dick Martin and Dan Rowan, who at the time were starring in the hit TV variety series "Laugh-In," were frisking Nat for the lost pen. Well, it made sense at the time.

$\int$ hort-budgeted photographic assignments meant no frills, no travel. The assignment was simply to get good photographs, under whatever circumstances prevailed. In short, create!

Here, in 1955, I found myself in the wilds of the Hollywood Hills, in the shadow of the Hollywood Sign, creating stills for a new "Tarzan" series that would feature the then-unknown muscleman/actor Gordon Scott. With Scott was his girlfriend, Vera Miles, one of Hollywood's established leading ladies. On this occasion, at least, Scott and Miles showed me that they, too, could ham it up.

Gordon Scott and Vera Miles

If you walked up Brooklyn's Amboy Street to the corner of Linden Boulevard and turned left, then continued on Linden Boulevard for about one mile, you would find yourself in Danny Kaye's old neighborhood and could even see the house he grew up in. To kids like me, who grew up in that section of Brooklyn in the 1930s and '40s, Danny Kaye was a hero. He was one of us, and he had made it! Danny Kaye's example gave every kid growing up in Brooklyn the hope that we too would somehow find the way out of our ghetto neighborhoods—Jewish, Italian, or African-American.

When I arrived in Hollywood in 1946, I soon found out that Danny Kaye was not the typical Hollywood movie star who would be seen frequently in the nightclubs and private parties around town. One rarely saw Danny and his wife, Sylvia Fine, at the usual filmland functions. I heard that, as entertainers go, the Kayes were considered recluses who infrequently left their Benedict Canyon home except for work, doctor visits, or flying lessons (like Robert Taylor, Kaye became a licensed pilot and flew his own plane). On rare occasions, they attended Hollywood functions such as charitable events or the Academy Awards. The rap on the Kayes was that they were really New York "theater people" and didn't want to get caught up in the Hollywood fluff.

My personal experiences with Danny Kaye were disappointing. Usually, after years of shooting actors and other show-business personalities, they would get to know me and behave, if not exactly like friends, at least less formally. So, I thought that after a while I would break through the rather cool and aloof distance that Danny Kaye kept from most people. But this never happened. It was difficult to imagine how Kaye could be such an outgoing, lovable, and warm performer at one moment and then, as soon as he was off stage or off camera, be transformed into what seemed like another person. When he was out on the town, he would pose for zany pictures with other celebrities and he seemed to be loving every moment of the publicity. But as soon as the last flash popped and the cameras stopped clicking, Kaye's other personality took over.

Danny Kaye taking a swing for the camera

Above:

Leslie Caron and puppets from Lili

Opposite:

Rock Hudson as Santa Claus, with Janet Leigh, Deborah Kerr, and Dean Martin

At the 1953 premier of the film Lili, in which she starred, French beauty Leslie Caron created a great "photo op" by planting a kiss on the cheek of one of the puppets that were used in the production. Photographers, hungry to come up with something that wasn't a typical premiere photo, loved this unique shot and jumped all over it.

Above:

Carmen Miranda

Opposite:

**Frank Sinatra hamming it up
in clown makeup for Betty
Hutton. Both were in
costume for the St. John's
Hospital benefit circus.**

Carmen Miranda was born in Portugal, but moved to Rio de Janeiro, Brazil, with her family when she was two. She grew up loving the music and dance that surrounded her in Brazil. She was discovered by Lee Schubert (of the famous theater family) in 1939. Schubert brought Miranda to the United States, where in record time she became a star.

Wearing her outrageous hats covered with fresh fruit, flamboyant gowns the likes of which had never been worn by stars in this country, and her platform shoes with wedge heels to add stature to her four-foot-eleven-inch frame, Carmen was quickly dubbed "The Brazilian Bomb Shell" and went on to star in every medium known to man in her era (1939 to 1955).

This photograph of Carmen Miranda, taken shortly before her untimely death from a heart attack in 1955, catches the firebrand energy she radiated. Whatever "it" was, Carmen Miranda had it. And back then, everyone loved "it."

Trigger and Bullet

Dale Evans was not a ham herself, and she generally stayed behind the scenes. But she created one of the funniest events in Hollywood each year when she made sure that Roy Rogers's horse Trigger would have a birthday party. Usually, caramel oats were served, along with fresh carrots, celery, and apples—all delicacies for equines. During and after their successful TV series, Dale and Roy would have their German shepherd dog Bullet at the coral, too, where he would share in the festivities.

Red Skelton with a puppy conga line: They say you should never follow a dog act. Classic ham Red Skelton would be a hard act to follow, with or without dogs.

Above:

Liberace cracking up Rosemary Clooney

Opposite:

Esther Williams in Sun Valley, offering a Coke to a snowman. Even the "million-dollar mermaid" liked to joke around.

On stage, Liberace was certainly the ultimate ham. He was also a nice guy who could be very funny in private. I don't know what the joke was here, but Rosemary Clooney was plainly having a good time with one of the twentieth century's great showmen.

At twenty-two I was still the new kid on the block as far as Hollywood's press photographers were concerned; most of my peers ranged from their thirties to their sixties. One night in 1948 I was assigned to cover a gigantic event, a charity circus to raise funds for St. John's Hospital in Santa Monica, California. The moguls of Hollywood worked very closely with the hospital and with the Ringling Brothers Barnum and Bailey Circus to gather together what seemed like every star in the Hollywood firmament to attend this event.

Bing Crosby, who was rather camera-shy, was one of the first stars to appear that evening. To my surprise and delight, he asked me to take a picture of him with Emmett Kelly, who at that time was the most famous circus clown in the world, and his friend, director John Farrow. There they were, three of the most famous people in show business, in casual dress, no costumes, no makeup, and no fright wigs or hair pieces. I thought, "What a scoop! My boss would love this." Bing Crosby, John Farrow, and Emmett Kelly each requested that I send them an 8 x 10 print, which I was happy to do. Then, feeling brave, I asked Crosby for a favor. He looked at me curiously and said yes. I asked him if he was really going to be made up as a clown, as I had heard him discussing with Emmett Kelly. He replied with another "Yep."

Now, pushing my luck, I asked if he would pose for me after he had been made up. Crosby thought for a hard moment and then gave me one of those looks that I recalled from his starring roles in *Going My Way* and *The Bells of St. Mary's* and said, "I'd love to, but it will cost you another 8 x 10."

I could hardly believe my good luck. One of the most hard-to-get subjects in Hollywood was asking *me* for a free 8 x 10! I was thrilled. Sure enough, about thirty minutes later a great-looking clown came up to me and asked, "Hey, son, are you ready?" I would never have recognized him by sight, but—that voice! It had to be, it was, Bing Crosby, and was I ever ready to shoot. I still cherish this photograph of Bing Crosby.

Bing Crosby as a clown at the St. John's Hospital benefit circus

Index

Front Endsheet:

Barbara Stanwyck, Glen Ford, and Van Heflin backstage. Verso: **Natalie Wood at age sixteen**

Back Endsheet:

William Holden, Jane Wyman, and Cary Grant at an evening event. Verso: **Jimmy Durante and his wife, Marjorie Little**

Editor: Elaine M. Stainton
Photo Editor: John Crowley
Designer: Maria L. Miller
Production Coordinator: Maria Pia Gramaglia

Library of Congress Cataloging-in-Publication Data

Garrett, Murray.
    Hollywood moments / text and photographs by Murray Garrett.
        p.   cm.
ISBN 0-8109-3242-3
    1. Motion picture actors and actresses–United States–Portraits.
I. Title. TR678 .G37 2002
791.43'028'092273–dc21

                                                                    2002002179

Copyright © 2002 Murray Garrett

Published in 2002 by Harry N. Abrams, Incorporated, New York
All rights reserved. No part of the contents of this book may be
reproduced without the written permission of the publisher.

Printed and bound in Japan
10 9 8 7 6 5 4 3 2 1

Harry N. Abrams, Inc.
100 Fifth Avenue
New York, N.Y. 10011
www.abramsbooks.com

Abrams is a subsidiary of
LA MARTINIÈRE
G R O U P E